Yesterdays

Childhood memoirs

By

Beverly Mattson Wheelhouse

and

Finished by her Granddaughter

Chelsy Wheelhouse Simerson

–1983–

CONTENTS

INTRODUCTION

Read this, my children, and you shall learn of life as it was when I was young; a simple life, there is no doubt by one filled with miracles, nonetheless.

The world was changing. Electricity! Tractors! Indoor facilities! Television! Jet airplanes! They all followed my arrival.

I was born on the edge of the great depression. A low point in this nation's history that no one, except the very wealthy escaped entirely. It was a time of hunger and despair. My story begins while the country is still in the recovery stage.

But this is not a story of depression, nor of sorrow. It is of a slower, happier time…….
My childhood.

HOME SWEET HOME

I was always happy in a cowboy hat

After my birth on January 8, 1934 in The Dalles, Oregon. My family brought me home to Sundale, Washington. My father was 34, my mother 28, and my sister, Denise, almost 5 years old. They had decided to keep me despite the fact I was a girl and hadn't fulfilled everyone's wishes. My birth occurred in the ninth year of my parents' marriage.

The family home was located near the middle of a plateau above and north of the Columbia River. To the west Rock Creek canyon divided us from the Goodnoe Hills Community. Chapman Creek stopped the plateau from continuing to the east. The Sundale Hills obscured any further view to the north. It was a treeless, windswept land, for the most part, with scant yearly rainfall.

A stranger passing through one hot summer day remarked he must have died and gone to hell. A native overheard him and replied, "Nope, you're wrong, stranger, this isn't hell….But you can see it from here." he added cheerfully.

Why this plateau received the name "The Burn" varies from family to family. Dad's theory was the Indians burnt the area each fall so the horses would have better grass the following year. This question is still debated whenever local historians gather.

My first home

It is forgotten how the name Sundale derived but one can imagine the person who originated the name did so on a hot sweltering August afternoon when the sun was topmost in his mind.

The folks probably received congratulations in the mail. Sundale's post office has mail delivered three times a week by a carrier who traveled to Sundale station to get it from the train. The mail was sorted in the store that had been in business for twenty years. Henry J.B. Meyers, the original owner, still ran it. He was our closest neighbor.

By the time of my arrival in Sundale, the community had

already withstood many changes. Wild horses had once roamed the open range but were now all but fenced off from The Burn. Orchards had been planted and died from lack of water. Many homesteads had flourished briefly but were now bought up by the few landowners who remained. Sheep ranches were on their way to extinction with only three or four remaining from perhaps a dozen which once thrived in the area.

Teddy & I at the Hayes Place (Cellar in back ground) This is the era when Mom caught me stuffing silverware thro a hole in the floor there.

Limited wheat farming had taken place as early as the 1890's on The Burn. It was this occupation the people reverted to following the orchard boom and bust.

Dad farmed land leased from Dan Horrigan, a wealthy Seattlite who bought thousands of acres from Horse Heaven to The Burn in the 1920's and 1930s. People were discouraged from dust blows and depression prices from their crops; for some, the banks' foreclosure meant an end to their farming dreams. Whenever these farms came up for sale, Dan was there with his checkbook. He needed young ambitious men to run these farms for him. Dad was anxious to oblige.

So, my destiny was shaped even before I left the
hospital that winter of 1934.

I was a farm girl.

Older sister Denise (7) & Me (2)~

THE OTHER FAMILY

As a family, we were seldom alone. So many people worked at the ranch it is impossible to remember them all. Their names are listed in Dad's time ledgers that date from 1937 thou their faces are blurred in memory.

Marilynn, Denise, Joe Luis and me

Grandpa Clyde Davenport lived with us while he was on the payroll from March 1937, and perhaps before, until November 1942. At this time it was discovered he had tuberculosis and was hospitalized. He died there sometime later from the disease. Grandpa Clyde's wheat ranch was one of those repossessed by the bank during the depression.

Another man who lost everything was Tom Rheam. After Dad had bought the Harrison Ridge property at a tax sale he learned the former owner had nowhere to go. Tom soon had permission to continue living in his log cabin until better times arrived. He cut firewood and did seasonal work for us for years. There were many destitute men on the road in those days who felt fortunate to receive three square meals

a day and a place to sleep. Their paycheck was just a bonus
to them.

In the early 1940's, a man brought his wife and small
son to live in a tent they pitched on the front lawn while
he worked in the harvest fields.
An unforgettable hired man was Dad's first cousin,

Ivan Mattson, Burton Wiideanen, ?Bean?, Fred Davenport & Dad

Burton Wiideanean. He came to work in November of 1943 and
remained steady until the mid 50's. Burton's talent was
tractor driving or 'cat skinning'. Combines were still
being pulled by tractors during this era and Burton was one
of the best in this department.

Burton was a bachelor who usually remained on the ranch
on week-ends. On the infrequent times he went to town
Saturday night he sometimes 'forgot' to return on Monday.
This never happened when the work was urgent, however.

Burton was dependable when Dad needed him.

I never see a cherry pie but what thoughts of Burton come flooding back, even though this episode happened years ago. One evening, Mom placed one of her yummy cherry pies, hot from the oven, on the table. When Burton removed the first piece from the tin, hot juices flowed into the vacant space. He kept scooping the overflow onto his plate. We stared, open mouthed, as the pie grew thinner and thinner! A great deal of crust and very few cherries remained for the rest of us. After this, mom was careful to get the pies baked early so they'd be cool by supper time.

This is the way the cookhouse remained during the war.

Mom always had help with the cooking during harvest. A woman, listed in the ledger simply as 'cook', worked for 73 consecutive days in 1937 at $1.00 a day.

Dad began building a cook house in 1941. It had a bedroom, a middle kitchen and a dining room where we could gather for meals. The project came to a halt after the war started when building supplies became impossible to get. It was completed, finally, during the winter of 1946. A bathroom was added-on later.

While the cook house remained unfinished, the first full time cook was hired. Francis Miller and her daughter, Marilynn lived in one of our rooms upstairs. Marilynn became my best friend, mortal enemy and little sister all rolled into one. Despite our childhood squabbles, Marilynn became my favorite 'cousin' when Francis married Uncle Dick Mattson a few years later.

Grant and Lee Dorland were the first to live in the new cook house. She cooked for all of us, as the other cooks did. Grant was infatuated with the wild west. We never missed The Lone Ranger on the radio while he worked for us. Whenever a western was showing at the Star Theater in Goldendale, Grant and Lee would go. They always asked me to go and sometimes I did, if it was on a weekend. We saw Roy Rogers, Gene Autry, Jesse James and the Dalton Gang movies.

I loved westerns too.

We had fun with the hired men. Many of them had no families and I think enjoyed being in the midst of one. We learned to study the new help before playing the thumb-in-the-butter trick on them. There were some we thought wouldn't appreciate it so we left them alone. At least until we got to know them better. For those that don't know what the butter trick is, here is how the game is played. It is important to note that butter didn't come in neatly premeasured blocks for tubs with lids, back then. It was made in a butter churn, using milk from a cow that lived on the ranch. It was stored in a jar and portioned out onto a plate before each meal. When someone asked "please pass the butter", you would pass them the butter but right before they touched the plate you quickly moved the plate to catch their thumb in the butter. Most of the hired men were good sports and were included into the family leisure time. For example, whenever Joe Louis (a professional boxer) defended his championship there was someone to bet with. The men

Hired men who completed the cookhouse Harold Goff and Bob Schillings

wanted the challenger to win so I made-good in my early gambling endeavors as Louis was a champion for a long time.

In January of 1949, two young couples originally from Arkansas came to our door asking for work. It was the off season and we had no place for them to live so Dad was about to say "no" when Mom looked out the window and noticed one of the women holding a baby. Beyond a doubt they were broke and hungry and it appeared their old car would not go far. After the folds held a conference, Dad told them they were hired if they didn't mind the living quarters. These were the last people to live at the Hayes' and Peters' places. Both houses had been vacant for years and were in a bad state of disrepair; Neither had running water. Things went well until the morning of June 17th when the couple in the Hayes house discovered a rattlesnake crawling across the floor of the baby's room. The other couple stayed until seeding was finished that fall.

I don't know what determined the decision to keep a cook after harvest. Perhaps simply the fact she was a good one. One, I was relieved to find, was just summer help, who woke me up every morning so I could dump the garbage for her. Another woman boiled everything. I swear we ate boiled steak! Mrs. Nelson was steady help until she made the mistake of asking for a raise after the folks bought their first Buick. She said she hadn't realized they were so rich. Mom was so peeved, Mrs Nelson became one of the few who wasn't gifted with some of the unused treasures stored in the saddle shed when she left. I could cry when I think of the antiques Mom gave away. A set of amber depression glass dishes is just one of the things that came to mind that was given away.

Cupid was busy unleashing arrows around the ranch for a few years. While Daisy Barton worked for us her husband, Harley, was killed in a car wreck on lower Goodnoe grade. A few years later, she and Burton were married. Bob Schillings, a hired man who gave me my first airplane ride, married Jean Stout; and of course Ed Morris arrived in August of 1945, fresh from the air force, to eventually win Denise's heart.

All of these people helped enrich my life in some small way. It wouldn't have been the same without them. They truly were our "other" family.

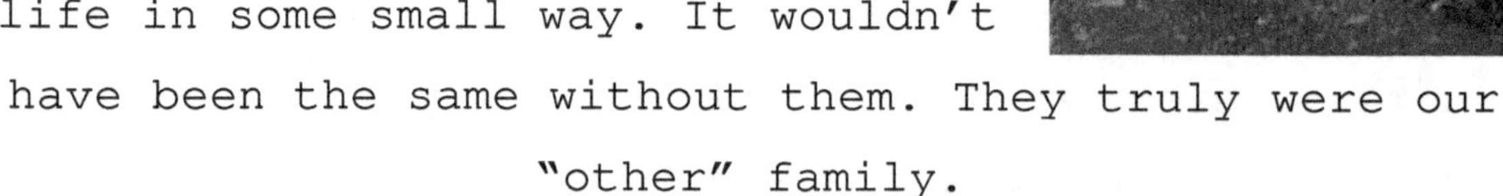

DAD BECOMES A CATTLEMAN

*Doin' a little cowboying on the way
to summer pasture ca 1950*

It was a new venture for both Dan Horrigan and Dad when they became partners in the cattle business in 1939. They traveled to Spokane to buy feeder calves. Curly Wade was hired as herdsman and a feedlot was built on the site we still use.

Curly batched at Grandpa Clyde's old house north of the feedlot. He remodeled the house extensively while he lived there. He evidently attended to his carpentry more than the cattle, for the first morning after the calves arrived, 5 were dead from foundering. One of these was Dad's milk cow's calf. Curly had put the calves on full feed immediately. The deaths that followed were attributed to

this mistake also. Dad soon took over as
manager.

A year or two later the partners
branched out into a cow-calf operation to
utilize the lush stand of bunch grass on
the Smythe Place. The partners traveled to
Canada and Montana to look at commercial
Hereford herds that were for sale. They
bought the Montana herd.

The cattle were kept at the Smythe
Place the first few years. Grant
Dorland lived at the ranch to feed and
help during calving. Branding took
place in the rickety corral that had
originally been built to hold sheep.

In a few years Dan became
discouraged with the profits from the
cattle business and offered his share
to Dad for $10,000. Dad accepted it. That fall he sold
calves and had only $2,500 left on the debt.

After Dad moved the cattle to the main ranch for the
winter he discovered the fences weren't tight enough to

keep the cattle in. Some were lost to the S.P.&S Railroad
when they wandered onto the tracks.

Dad gave Denise and I each a young cow with the
understanding we could keep any heifers that resulted until
our herd numbered 10. I named my cow Dot. My cattle herd
was literally cut in half when my first heifer calf, named
Double Dot, was one of those hit by the train. S.P.&S. sent
me a measly check for the damages. Dad was furious with the
amount but there was nothing to do but start over.

Dad would never let us get a job or even
work for wages on the ranch but he gave us
opportunities to make our own money. During the
war years I was in the hog business and made a
good profit. We sold the steer calves in the
fall. I opened a checking account at the Pioneer
State Bank in Goldendale when I was quite young, and felt
independently wealthy.

WORLD WAR TWO

December 7, 1941..Denise and I were awakened by a
worried looking mother who told us Pearl Harbor had
been bombed by the Japanese. I sat blinking my
eyes, wondering where Pearl Harbor was, who the
Japanese were and why was all of this concerning us?
It must be serious because Mom and Dad were upset.

As time went by I learned to call our foes
Japs and Krauts and booed them during the new reels
at the movies with the other kids. I bought 10
cent savings stamps at school and went to the old
school grounds several times a week where the

Today, because of growing environmental concerns, recycling is becoming more popular. But forms of recycling have always been part of the American scene, especially in times of crisis. During World War II, for example, when many goods were in short supply, ration stamps were a way of life and many items were recycled. Collections were held for tin cans, paper and even cooking grease. Old toothpaste tubes had to be turned in when buying new ones. Aluminum, used in aircraft construction, was an especially important item. Aluminum drives were common, and people considered it their patriotic duty to participate. Among the items collected in the nationwide drives were aluminum pots, pans and—the ultimate sacrifice—hair curlers.

entire student body had victory gardens. I didn't

understand how my short row of radishes was helping the war effort; and frankly, I still don't.

Whenever I rode in the family car I had to peer around a sticker which said "IS THIS TRIP REALLY NECESSARY?" On the other side of the windshield was an A sticker, which meant we had top priority for gas as we were farmers.

It seemed there were ration stamps for everything, including sugar, coffee, meat, tires, and shoes. It was the latter that caused me the most distress.

Me and my pretty red sandals~

Mom would take me to Ledbetter's Department Store where I'd bear the dreaded words, "Beverly wants a pair of sturdy shoes." I did not want a pair of sturdy shoes and I'd do my best to point out pretty sandals like I used to wear. Mom would not be swayed. These shoes must last until the next stamps were issued..so sturdy they were. Even Mr. Ledbetter's gift of a Buster Brown balloon or a Poll Parrot clacker didn't help to raise my spirits after these shopping trips.

If Mom had done the hiring of the harvest crew in those days, I'm sure the only credentials she'd have asked for was if they had brought their sugar stamps. She canned dozens of quarts of fruit each year besides baking for the crew, who more times than not didn't bring their stamps. We suffered through sugarless cakes, Pies that were never sweet enough and worst of all no Kool-AID!

Denise (15) and Me (10) 1

She finally had an idea of filling a pint jar of sugar for everyone on Sunday. These sat on the table next to each plate and was supposed to last all week. This was done mainly because one hired man used 3 heaping teaspoons of sugar in every cup of coffee. I couldn't help thinking he wasn't a good American but by the end of each week I was sharing my sugar with him.

The Smythe Ranch was some distance from home and created a problem because of the gas shortage. It was decided to move there so Mom and Francis Miller could cook for the harvest crew to eliminate so much travel.

Dan Horrigan had bought the old sheep ranch in 1939 so the house had been vacant for several years. Francis and

Denise were sent up early to do some house cleaning. While they were occupied with their work 2 training planes flew over shooting blanks at one another. I imagine the war seemed very close to them that day. The planes would occasionally overrun the boundary of the bombing range in the east. Dad picked up brass cartridges from fields for years.

It was quite a job to move. A truck was filled with furniture plus everything we'd need for the stay. Even the milk cow went. Marilynn, Francis's daughter, and myself had imagined all kinds of adventures playing on the bluff in back of the house. Our hopes were crushed when we were told not to go far because there were too many rattlesnakes around. Luckily, I had brought several Nancy Drew books, so I spent most of my time on the front porch reading.

Conditions were primitive at the Smythe Ranch even to our standards in those days. There was no kerosene refrigerator, only a screened cooler jutting from the pantry wall to the outside. A hand pump in the kitchen provided water from the well. It was here someone discovered a dead mouse floating around one day. Maybe this was the reason we moved there for just one year. It was a headache for everyone.

During the first
summer of the war there
was a shortage of grain
sacks. This was serious as
the wheat was still
sacked. Dad made a table
from planks and barrels
and paid Denise 5 cents
for

~ Mom, and the car ca. 1940~

each sack she patched with pieces of burlap and glue. I
wanted to help but was told I was too young. I spent those
days nearby, making mud pies and giving her moral support.

Mother heard somewhere the country needed recycled tin
cans. We began washing, peeling labels and flattening all
the cans we used. Here was something I could do! I
flattened cans with gusto all summer. The soles of my
sturdy shoes became a bit threadbare from it all.

~ Me wearing sturdy shoes~

I sat in the back seat with my squashed treasures neatly stacked in boxes around me on the day we took them to town. The question was…where do we deliver them? We couldn't find any place in Goldendale to leave them. We brought them home and unceremoniously threw them in the dump. Thank god every American's war effort wasn't as futile as mine… it is doubtful we'd have won.

We received the Life Magazine in the mail each week. Issues full of gruesome war pictures that made us thankful we lived where we did and sorry for the people involved in the war.

Toward the end of the war, I was playing on the hay pile one evening when 16 brown bombers flew over. They were low and going so slow they seemed tired. We were all tired of the war. How happy we were to hear it was all over!

SPRINGTIME ON THE RANCH

Spring time was when dreaded, long cotton stockings were tucked deep into the bottom dresser drawer and meadowlarks sang cheerful songs from fencerows and dust storms and baby chicks arrived.

One of my chores was to feed the chickens and gather eggs from the hen house. This was then time of year to alert Mom when a broody hen refused to leave the nest because she might be a candidate to hatch some eggs. After two or three days and the hen was still determined to hang

~Denise with her Madame
Alexander
& Me with Mr. Five bv

tight despite my discouragement, Mom would join me in the hen house to inspect her. If the hen filled the requirements of a red comb, had size enough to cover a nest of eggs and was crankier than a basket of rattlesnakes, she was introduced to a wooden apple box filled with straw and eggs and placed in the grainery. Here she would remain for the next 21 days, being fed and watered daily and sitting like a lump on her nest.

When the first chicks arrived they were brought to the house in a cardboard box and placed near a sunny window to wait for their siblings to hatch. If this wasn't done the hen might leave the next before all the eggs hatched. The chicks ate mashed, boiled eggs, shells and all, offered to them in zinc canning lids. Their favorite form of recreation was escaping from the box. It seemed there was always one to catch. Even though they were cute and fuzzy, it was a relief when they were placed with their mother in the coup under the locust trees near the hen house. They were confined here until they were old enough to escape the hooves of the barn yard animals.

Because the road in front of the house was a state highway in those days, more traffic went by than now. Among the more interesting passers-by were the sheep shearers. Their hand-made homes nailed to pickups and trucks were a most unusual sight. They made a caravan of up to ten vehicles some years.

A few days after the shearers had gone by, we began watching for Horace White's bands of sheep who were trailed by on their trek to Mt. Adams for the summer. After all the expectations of waiting for the sheep to appear, the best part was the dogs. They were so clever, darting everywhere, nipping the right ewe every time. I wondered how they kept up their frantic pace all day. A herder, leading his horse, brought up the rear. Then they were gone until fall.

The only event to surpass the sheep exodus was the Indian Root Festival. For a few days, traffic was heavy, heading for the long house at Rock Creek. No matter how chilly the weather, the squaws and children rode in the back of the pickups.

We always went to the Pow-Wow, but one year Chief Willie Yallop himself came to the house to invite us as special guests. The long house was a huge canvas tent, erected in the village especially for the event.

We arrived earlier than usual that year and enjoyed watching the squaws play the stick game. Shiny silver dollars changed hands rapidly. I wanted to learn the game but Mom shook her head. We were allowed to bet on Joe Louis's fights on the radio or make Presidential election wagers but the stick game was too much like gambling!

When we stepped inside, it took a while for our eyes to become adjusted to the darkness. Kerosene lanterns were lit but failed to illuminate the large interior brightly. Around the perimeter of the then, bedrolls were tucked neatly out of the way. As the evening progressed and one grew tired, all that had to be done was to unroll the bed and go to sleep. Some did! A marvel, considering the drums and the singers who chanted almost constantly.

There were many people there we knew, but a lot of strangers too, for the Yakima tribe had seven branches who were all represented. Indians from other tribes were present too.

I spotted some of my Indian school mates who said "Hi", but didn't ask me to join in their play. Johnny Barney, who built fence for Dad occasionally, was one of the drummers. He was best known, however, for his singing ability. Whenever Johnny sat at our table, he hardly ever spoke and then barely above a whisper. I supposed he was saving his vocal chords. He could wail with the best of them at the pow-wow.

When Chief Yallop entered the tent, he walked to his bedroll to change his costume. He peeled right down to his long underwear! I didn't think this was a chiefly thing to do, even though the tent was dimly lit.

The main event of the root festival was the dancing which took place every night. When the drumming began only a few dancers were ready for the first dance. More dancers gradually appeared and soon the tent was ablaze with beautiful costumes made of buckskins, real eagle feathers and adorned with meticulous beadwork. All ages were represented on the hard packed dirt floor, from the oldest squaw, wrapped tightly in her fringed shawl to the tiniest warrior, who stole the scene until Gus made his appearance.

Gus George, who later became chief at Rock Creek, was one of the rare men who wore braids in those days. When he finally arrived to dance everyone took notice! He wore heavy bells around his ankles that precisely matched the drum beat with every step. Gus was a joy to watch, even though people said he was past his prime and not the dancer he once was.

During the evening, Dad was escorted to the center of the tent, where he was presented a beautiful pair of fringed, beaded buckskin gloves. I learned later that he had loaned the tribe $100 to put on the festival after the Pioneer State Bank in Goldendale had refused to help them.

There were some who drank too much firewater during the

event. It was a rare year when Dad didn't have to repair the bull pasture fence along Walker Grade where some careening vehicle hit it. Once a jeep load of jolly over inhibitors drove by war chanting at the top of their lungs to the accompaniment of a drum. It made goose bumps on our arms, even though we knew the Indians were friendly.

Checking the fence around the Smythe Place with Dad before we took the cows to summer pasture was a chore I enjoyed. Tom Miller's property touched ours on three sides. We counted 96 horses along his fence line one year. All but 5 or 6 were working horses.

With the exciting springtime event out of the way, life became moresimple. Lying in the barn window on a windy day watching the clouds form imaginable scenes or dropping wisps of hay through cracks in the grainery loft, hoping to score a bullseye on the lump in the apple box below, were some of our quiet pastimes.

In late spring began the agony of waiting for the sweet cherries to ripen. If wishing had made it so, the fruit would have been ready three weeks early.

SUMMER TIME

Summer days were long on the ranch. As our bedroom was off the dining room, Denise and I were usually awakened by the crew pulling their chairs up to the breakfast table. More times than not we were dressed and had taken our places at the table by the time they had finished their cereal. I always hoped they had eaten it all but it never happened, Mom cooked plenty of oatmeal.

Bobby Carl and I in doorway of playhouse

We cleared the table after each meal which didn't take long because of THE LAW. If anyone forgot to take his plate to the kitchen on their way out he was fined $.25. The person discovering the forgotten plate received the quarter. We collected often enough to keep it interesting.

The first thing I bought with my treasured quarters was a cream pitcher for Mom in the shape of Elsie the cow. Denise helped make out the order from the catalog. The morning after the pitcher arrived she was filled with cream and put on the table. Whenever Elsie was used a drop of cream would run down her chin, across the daisy garland on her neck, under her tummy and drip off her tits onto the table. The men laughed and called her an easy milker. I was so embarrassed! After the men had gone, Mom said she'd use the pitcher for Dad's coffee cream during the day. Elsie spent many years on day duty in the kerosene refrigerator.

Honey Bunny & I in the phlox bed

Air conditioning was far in the future. There were several places one could go to get relief from the heat but they were almost all forbidden. One of my favorite places was the rickety wood shed whose roof brushed the limbs of one of the many locust trees that surrounded the yard. It was nice to lay on the roof among the leaves pretending it was Tarzan's home. I ran a nail in my foot there once but I suffered in silence because I shouldn't have been there.

The cellar was another cool spot. Even though it was dimly lit and spidery I longed to sit there, but couldn't.

I never knew why unless Mom was afraid some of the jars of food on the shelves would be broken.

The best place was under the green water wagon Dad had drug into the yard to use as a reserve water supply when the pipeline sprang a leak. The wagon was antique enough to have several slow drips. It was always damp and cool underneath. Mom didn't trust it…she expected the splintery old wood to explode any second. I was really in TROUBLE if I was caught under it; and I was, more than once. That left running through the sprinkler on the lawn the only cool, legal pastime we had.

Meanwhile, on the hot blistering days, Mom was in the kitchen with the wood stove burning, canning fruits and vegetables that couldn't wait for a cooler day. She'd send us to the cellar for empty jars. We were glad to go, not only to get cooled off, but to admire the strange gadgets stored there. The lard press, the bottle capper and other things we didn't understand always got our attention.

While on one of these jar errands, we decided to explore a far corner. I had just crawled into the large wooden bin to see what was there when Mom's shout, "Girls I need those jars right now!", sent us scurrying up to the kitchen. Mom took one look at me and shrieked, "Beverly! What were you doing in the coal bin?!" I was black from head to foot. I began to understand why the cellar was off limits. There were too many things for a curious child to get into down there.

Marilynn and I became journalists one summer when we published a handwritten weekly paper. The news consisted of such items as; GINGER HAD THREE KITTENS IN THE BARN THE DAY BEFORE YESTERDAY, WE THINK THE FATHER IS NIGGY. The hired men were good sports to read it but we sometimes wondered why they laughed. Didn't they realize this was serious stuff?

The number of plates on the table grew considerably during harvest time. The men were housed in a building in the barnyard. It was sparsely furnished with iron beds and a wood heating stove. Orange crates served as nightstands and wall shelves. We were never allowed to go near the place without Mom. When she changed the sheets we'd tag along, mainly to get a quick glance at the "Police Gazettes" and "Ranch Romance" magazines or to admire the scantily dressed women on the calendars. Mom would hurry us out the door.. boy, she could change beds fast!

Wash benches for the crew stood near the standpipe in the backyard. They were equipped with wash pans, lava soup and scratchy linen towels. Dad built a shower stall near the bunk house with a barrel on top that was filled with water every morning. If the sun had shone that day the men could take a lukewarm shower before supper. It was amazing how many of them chose not to use it often enough.

~Dads First Tractor~

As summer progressed and feed ran out of Rock Creek, the wild horses migrated to The Burn. The horses milled around on the west side of the store before daring to make a dash past the buildings. This gave me time to lock Joe Louis (my dog) in the wash house and take my stand behind the biggest locust tree next to the road. Very seldom was the herd made up of the same horses entirely. Sometimes there were as many as 25 in the bunch; rarely less than ten. Some of these horses belonged to the Indians who lived at the creek. These were the leaders who looked for ways into the wheat fields. When Dad or one of the neighbors discovered the herd in their field, they'd chase the horses back down Walker Grade at full speed.

As if the folks didn't have enough to handle during these tedious harvest days, the relatives chose now to visit. The older cousins with Denise would ride Sam (the horse) and the milk cow's calf (on the sly) and play monopoly for hours. Younger girl cousins played paper dolls and made mud pies with me in the play house. Young boy cousins caused some disturbances by teasing us, but we had good times.

*Denise, Me, Marilynn and cousins
Joannie and David*

*Aunt Gladys Tallman Jim, Del, Sis and I
at Wishram*

FALL OR BUTCHERING TIME

Fall found the hectic days of harvest over. After the seeding was in and the crew thinned, the folks had some leisure time. This did not necessarily mean a vacation, however, as the only one we ever took was to San Francisco for the World's Fair in 1939. Leisure time for the folks meant Dad could repair machinery and Mom could do some heavy house cleaning that was often neglected during busy times.

Hog butchering time arrived after the nights became frosty. The flies were gone and the days remained chilly so the meat kept cool. There was no electricity on the ranch so this was important.

Ed Morris & Uncle Ivan cutting up pork

The old Nichols Shepard steam engine was fired to heat water to fill the large vats used to scald the carcasses.

There is an old adage saying everything is used from the hog except the squeal. We never even heard the squeal because Mom found some excuse to visit a neighbor when that dreadful time arrived. We were always taken along and returned in time to watch the scraping of the hides.

Ed & Burton

The next week was a busy one! Dad cut up the hogs and made sausage with the hand operated meat grinder. The chops and roasts were wrapped and taken to Goldendale to the frozen meat lockers at the Reliance Creamery.

The hams and bacon were placed into wooden barrels

along with a salt brine strong enough to float a potato. Later, brown sugar and probably other ingredients were added before the meat was strung up in the smoke house to be cured. Most years the procedure was successful; on others, Mom par-boiled the meat to remove the excess salt before cooking it. Nothing was wasted on the ranch, so we ate it, even though we'd rather not. One couldn't always trust a potato for accuracy.

After the sausage was ground it was seasoned with Mom's special blend of sage and other herbs. What we didn't use right away was formed into patties, fried, then packed into quart jars, covered with rendered fat and canned in the pressure cooker. This shelf, in the cellar, was the first to be emptied. Sausage was popular at our house.

Pigs knuckles were boiled until tender, put in a crock with a pickling solution, then placed in the closet under the stair where it was cool. Several weeks went by before they were ready. Under the fat and spices was a treat worth all the wait. Mom sometimes served these as a side dish for meals. We were delighted if any of the hired men passed the plate without taking one…it meant more for us. Even so the pig's knuckles mysteriously disappeared before I'd had my fill. I suspect Mom liked them even better than I did.

When Dad removed the huge cast iron kettle and lard
press from the cellar, we knew it was time to render the
fat into lard. This was my favorite event of butchering
time. I'd sit on a block of wood near the fire to keep Dad
company while he stirred the chunks of fat in the kettle.
When the chunks were cooked, the rendered fat was dipped
from the kettle into coffee cans. What remained of the
chucks were squeezed through the lard press which turned
them into disc shaped masses called cracklings. We used the
cracklings as snacks for our chubby black cocker spaniel,
Joe Louis. The lard was stored in the cellar to be used for
pie crust and cooking oil.

One of the pig's bladders was always saved. This was
inflated and hung on the clothes line to dry. We batted it
around like a volleyball for a few days, then forgot about
it. Joe Louis was usually the last to be seen with it,
dragging it to the orchard to be buried in his bone yard.

~Dads first steam tractor~

We enjoyed watching the Canadian geese fly over each fall. One day the sky over the house was black with them. Grandpa Clyde called us out so we wouldn't miss the spectacle. Dad didn't hunt then, but when they got too thick in the green wheat, he'd shoot at them with the rifle to scare them away. We ate goose occasionally, if he was lucky enough to "scare" one in the head.

Sometimes on Sundays we'd travel to Centerville to visit Grandpa and Grandma Mattson. Almost every farm near Centerville still had a hay derrick in those days. It was the wrong time of year to see them in action but they were fascinating and fun to count as we drove along.

*My Grandparents and Uncle Dick lived west of town several miles on land great-grandfather Lars had homesteaded in 1876. As the original Victorian home had burnt not too many years before, their house was relatively new. They even had an indoor bathroom! The door was always kept closed though and I was disappointed to find it almost as cold as our outhouse.

By the time I started to school we too, had indoor plumbing but I remember using the chamber pot at night and the privy by day. We took baths in the kitchen in the round galvanized tub with water heated in the reservoir on the side of the cook stove.

In late fall the Christmas catalogs arrived in the mail. We did most of our shopping from them. There was a great deal of whispering and deep dark secrets in the next few weeks. We were so excited about the upcoming holiday we never realized, or cared, when fall ended and winter began.

WINTER

Snow is the most important ingredient of winter for a child. It floated down from above for your exclusive use to build snowmen or simply for the pleasure of tracking it up.

Another important ingredient is a sledding hill, which we didn't have; nevertheless, Dad made a wooden sled for me. Joe Louis didn't appreciate my efforts to train him as a sled dog so I just drug it along behind. Sometimes the men would take pity on me and we'd take a flying trip through the barn yard but this happened far too seldom.

We opened our presents on Christmas Eve. One year I got a toy sewing machine that really stitched. Never caring much for dolls, making clothes for them didn't interest me. I discovered Mom's sewing box full of socks to be patched. I stitched the tops of the socks together very neatly. I learned to remove stitches that year too.

~Joe Louis & I....Tracking snow~

If the present I had wanted for Christmas wasn't under the tree I had another chance as my birthday is January 8th. I never felt deprived for having a birthday so close to Christmas. My cake always had pink frosting. I was intrigued how red food coloring turned pink in powdered sugar icing so I asked for it every year.

Winter nights were spent playing games by the light of a kerosene lamp. We played authors, pit and old maid. As I grew older I joined the Monopoly and Chinese checker games.

The kerosene lamp played a part in making me beautiful. Mom placed the curling iron in the chimney to heat it, then she'd wrap it briefly around each lock…like magic, my hair curled or later braided. I hated sitting still for both.

On exceptionally cold nights, Mom heated said irons on the stove, wrapped them carefully in many thicknesses of newspapers and towels and put them in our bed so we could warm our feet. It seemed they would eventually end up on Denise's side of the bed but after putting my cold feet on her she'd become more generous and pushed them to my side for a while. It was nice to have a big sister to sleep with, especially in winter. Later, when she moved upstairs to her own room, I missed her.

Along with the cook stove in the kitchen, the house was

warmed by a heating stove placed midway between the living and dining rooms. Before going to bed, Dad would shovel in some coal so the fire would burn all night. Mom didn't like the smell or the dust that coal created so wood was used during the day.

If we were awake before the men came for breakfast, we'd grab our clothes and run in by the stove to dress. After the first burn on your backside one learned not to bend over to tie a shoe while standing too close to the stove. There were some hazards involved but worth the risk as the alternative was dressing in a cold room.

I practiced music lessons more faithfully in winter. Doing jigsaw puzzles, listening to the radio or reading occupied much of our time. We had a crank style phonograph upstairs. The needle was changed and the machine cranked before every song. There were piles of old records to play. My favorites were "The Wheel of the Wagon is Broken" by Patsy Montana and "The girls ARE fat as Pigs in Kansas".

In time, even a child grows tired of snow. The thrill of seeing the first gold star daisy meant winter was nearly over and yellow bells, shooting stars and violets would soon be blooming along Walker Grade.

So the seasons made their circle year after year; each

one bringing new discoveries of this wonderful world around
me.

DAYS ON THE RANCH

On the rare days when nothing was happening on the ranch, it might be livened up by the appearance of Archie Averill in his Shell gas truck. We would lean against the barnyard fence; or if Mom wasn't looking, climb on the wood shed to watch him maneuver the fuel barrels.

Mr. Lundberg, the Watkins man, might also pay a visit, which was more exciting because he always left a gift. It might be just a sample can of ointment or cough syrup, but sometimes it was gum so it was worth hanging around for.

Me, Mom & Denise

At least once during the summer, Wes Miller came jangling down the road in his wagon pulled by a team of horses. He would stop to water the horses and say hello to Francis, who was related to him somehow. He had a peg leg and reminded me of an old sea captain. He was on his way to visit his brother, Tom, who lived eight miles or so to the east.

Traveling salesmen would drop in occasionally at meal time. Mom would set another plate at the table and charge him 50 cent. One man who had car trouble and spent the night gave Denise and I birthstone rings. Hers was a purple amethyst and mine a dark red garnet. I enjoyed reading the tiny letters inside the band that said 10K. I was sorry when I lost the ring years later as it was the only birthstone I ever owned.

Gus and Raleigh Beeks would stop to chat if someone was in the yard when they rode by on horseback. Gus had a pet crow that flew along beside him. One day I caught the bird coyly hiding my rubber snap blocks under the lawn turf. I never trusted him after that. It was claimed he could talk but I never heard anything beyond a raspy caw. Still, it was neat to own a pet crow and I wanted one too.

Sometimes we'd go up to the store to buy penny candy or a dam bar. The latter must have commemorated Grand Coulee because the wrapper read, "The best bar by a dam site". They were my favorite. If we were lucky someone might pull in to buy gas while we were there. Johnnie or Cy Beeks would unlock the pump door and pull the lever back and forth until the gas reached the amount the person wanted in the glass globe on top. Then it disappeared through the hose into the car's gas tank. We might buy a box of cracker

jacks that contained a nice prize in those days. I hoped
for a China doll about three inches high or a tin whistle
that got everybody's attention when it was blown. This
somehow reminds me of my jews harp.

There were times when Dad and the
crew worked in the shop where the forge,
hand drill, anvils and other tools were
kept. I would lean in the doorway and
entertain them with concerts on my jews
harp. It came up missing one day. I
think someone who didn't appreciate my
musical talent mercifully placed it on a
dusty rafter out of the way.

I learned to run the forge. Dad reminded me each time
that a smooth slow crank was better than the fast start I
usually gave it. It created sparks and burnt the coal too
fast but was more exciting.

The magnet always fascinated me. The best game with it
was to scoop up metal shavings beneath the drill and place
them on a paper. By running the magnet underneath the
paper, squadrons of pretend soldiers marched to my command.

Denise with Butch, Me with braids, Bobby Carl and sturdy shoes

Some more entertaining games were trying to bury grasshoppers under wheat kernels and rubbing Mormon crickets noses together, then watching them fight.

Any peaceful day could be interrupted by the appearance of a rattlesnake. Mom glanced out the window one day and saw a large one crawling across the front porch. The porch floor forevermore carried the scars of the hoe she used to kill it with.

TRIPS TO TOWN

I may have been a farm girl but when we went to town I didn't look the part. Mom dressed us like we were going to a party and in a way it seemed like one.

~Denise & I, ready for town~

There were two ways to travel to Goldendale in those days; through Goodnoe Hills or up Rock Creek. The folks preferred the creek road. Depending on the season the creek had a variety of sights.

In the spring, bands of sheep at the Jess Imerie and Rollo Jackson ranches were kept near the road. Dad hated sheep, (even before he became a cattleman) and it had rubbed off onto me, but I had to admit the frisky lambs with their long funny tails were cute to watch.

In the winter, government mules were pastured at the creek. The mules were used by the forest service in the summer as pack animals. Dad said they were branded with

U.S. on their sides. We hoped they were close to the road so we could see for ourselves. From the first I'd heard about the Battle of Little Bighorn I had been a Custer freak. This was the same brand Comanche had worn. Wow!

I prayed the folks wouldn't have time to stop for a visit with Jess and Helen Imerie on this trip. Not that I didn't like them; it was their three boys I could miss seeing. I didn't care much for the swinging bridge we had to walk across either. It was to the bridge the boys enticed me one day on the pretense they had something neat to show me. When in the middle of the span I realized they weren't following. They began jumping at their end, causing the bridge to sway alarmingly. My screams finally brought Helen and Mom from the house to rescue me. On other visits I was chased with fence posts and knives. Marion, the youngest, tried to help me at times, but he was too small to conflict much damage to his big brothers.

Half way up Rock Creek grade a spring leaked out of the bank. Someone had inserted a pipe in it so water ran slowly out onto the ground through it. A tin cup hung on the pipe. We often stopped to get a cool drink or fill the car's radiator on a hot day.

A favorite crawdad hole at the bottom of the grade brought pleas of "Let's stop a while" whenever we drew near. If there was time to spare we'd tease the crawdads with a stick, until they grew mad enough to grab ahold, then we'd try to flip them onto the bank. They always escaped but we didn't care; it was just fun getting your hands wet and watching the creek flow by. The folks lived in a tent on this site in their early marriage while Dad worked for the County Highway Department. We were amazed at pictures in the family album that proved this was true.

The ride through Pleasant Valley was, strangely enough, pleasant. It was here Mom had spent her growing up years. She pointed out the spot where she had been born in 1905. Nothing remained on the site but two large poplar trees. The house her family had lived in later was still there, and is yet today. I always wanted to see the inside but as she didn't know the people living there it was out of the question. The school she had attended was now a grange hall.

As we approached Goldendale the snowcapped peaks of Mt. Hood, Mt Adams and Mt. St. Helens would suddenly come into view. Mom had told us Mt. St. Helens would erupt again someday so whenever we noticed wisps of clouds above it we asked if it was erupting. We were relieved when the answer was "No". In the summer after some of the snow had melted off the rocks, Mom would try to point out the figure 5 on

Mt. Adams' slopes. Despite my active imagination it was impossible for me to claim I could distinguish it. I took her word for it was up there…somewhere.

About this period during our trips one of the little voices from the back seat would cry out "I see Goldendale!" It was a game we played to see who could spot town first.

We seldom ate in town but when we did it was at the Simcoe Cafe. If halibut was on the menu, Mom ordered it. I didn't understand her attraction for the smelly stuff. I usually had a hot roast beef or turkey sandwich swimming in gravy with a strawberry ice-cream cone for dessert. While waiting for our meal we played stack hands. The game was played with everyone alternating their hands in a pile on the top, going faster and faster until the stack was hopelessly toppled and we girls had the giggles. It was a silly game but kept us from remembering how hungry we were.

The folks bought their groceries at Bert Sanders' Red and White store. Our piano was bought from Bert, after he had been given it as a payment for a grocery bill during the depression. He told Dad it had once belonged to the Golden family, whom the town had been named after. The grocery list was handed to one of the clerks who filled the order then packed it neatly in wooden boxes for the trip home. A vanilla but Smith's gave a premium of a knick knack with theirs. The poor Watkins man lost sales as there was usually something on the shelf one of us wanted and the only way to get it was to buy a bottle of vanilla.

After Bert sold his business, we patronized Bates' grocery. Here a cart was provided and one gathered their own supplies. Mr. Bates gave us a piece of salt water taffy when we left. I think Bert had given us a sucker.

My favorite place was Knox's 5 & 10 cent store. Mr. Knox supplied me with such necessities as paper dolls, color crayons and chalk for years. His candy counter was the best in town but I refrained; mainly because I was still savoring what the grocery man had given me. Sometimes I purchased a package of Sen-Sen to enjoy later.

While I was in the music phase of my life, Biggs Music Shop replaced the 5 & 10 Cent store as my favorite business. We bought sheet music here and sometimes, records. Mr. Biggs played the records we were interested in, then we could decide to buy or not. His record player was a fancy model run by electricity; lucky for him, as his arms would have gotten tired using one like ours. He might have even had to put his pipe down to make a sale: he was never without it.

There was a soda fountain in Allison's Pharmacy where

we bought strawberry sodas or a cherry coke on the rare times we went there. The folks did their business at McKee's Drug Store across the street but sometimes Mom had shopping to do for the hired men or cooks who had gotten their subscriptions at Allison's. These purchases were entered in Dad's time book and settled up at the end of the month.

No trip to town was complete unless we had gone to McKenzie Hardware. I loved to wander through the aisles wondering how some of the articles were used. It sort of reminded me of our cellar.

The last stop of the day was at the Reliance Creamery to pick up some frozen meat from the locker. This is why we took heavy coats to wear even on the hottest days. The meat was carefully wrapped in blankets in the car. This was a perplexing matter; you wrapped in a blanket to get warm, not to stay cold. It was another one of those childhood mysteries!

Reliance Creamery & Cold Storage Plant, Goldendale Wash.

It was at the creamery where I tasted my first soft ice cream. It was rich and creamy. I couldn't complain that vanilla was the only flavor available. The creamery proudly displayed a plaque on the wall stating they had won an award for their butter. I thought we should buy some to see if it was as good as they claimed but we never did. Mom churned her own butter.

A trip to town on the alternate route meant fording Rock Creek. If the water was high one traveled a half mile further to cross the bridge at Canapos. Mom miscalculated the ford one day and found herself stuck. We three trudged up Walker grade for help.

This is probably why the folks preferred the creek road.

HORSES_HORSES_HORSES

Dad bought his first tractor in 1935, the year after I was born so I missed the era of the workhorse; however, he had kept his favorite team who were enjoying their retirement loafing in the pasture.

One Saturday, after I had started to school, Dad hitched Pat and Mike to an old hack and asked if I wanted to go along to the bull pasture to help repair fences. This was an exciting event as I had never seen the horses in harness before. On the way home,

The team and I ca. 1940

after a little coaching, Dad handed the reins to me. It was the only time I drove a team.

At the age of four I tumbled off old Sam and got caught in the mouth by a flying hoof that knocked out my front teeth. Mom discouraged horse activities for me after this incident.

It wasn't until I became friends with a new girl at school that my interest in horses was renewed. Her name was Nancy Stout. She lived six miles away at the Shattuck, or Gately Place as it was known then.

After Sam kicked my teeth out, I didn't smile for the camera til new ones came in.

One Saturday Nancy rode her Mother's horse over for a visit. Chief was a big, ugly roan gelding covered with hip and shoulder brands. He even had a star brand on his cheek. When I mentioned it, Nancy explained it was an Indian brand and continued with a story that changed my life.

Chief had once been a wild horse who ranged in the Horse Heaven Hills. For years men tried to catch him. Indians finally captured him using a relay method where a series of horses with riders ran him down. Chief was too old to be trained easily so the Indians became discouraged and beat him. When this only made matters worse, he was sold. It seemed this horse would never submit to man as he was sold again and again; each owner appling their brand.

It was obvious he was an outlaw by the time Nancy's mother bought him. With patience and kindness he turned into a good saddle horse. Even in his old age Chief could run like the wind.

What an exciting story! From that day on horses fascinated me.

Poor old Sam had to put up with me again. I read "The Black Stallion" and "My Friend Flicka" series. My room was decorated with pictures of horses cutout of the "Western Livestock Journal" magazine. I bought a cowboy hat, sturdy western boots (no more sandals for me), and wore levis so tight they were uncomfortable, although I'd never have admitted it.

When Nancy moved only a half mile away, to the old Counts place, things got even worse. Our goal in life was to have a ranch in Texas. We went around trying to yodel like Patsy Montana, much to the distress of our families.

Not long after this transformation of my personality, an Indian who owed Dad $10.00 appeared with a bay filly. We unloaded her in the lane, avoiding flying hooves. It was easy to see she was no pampered pet. We turned her loose in the barnyard and leaned against the gate to watch. Suddenly she came dashing back to the gate and stopped to smell my arm. We both stood shivering with excitement for a few seconds before she ran off. The Indian turned to Dad and said, "She's going to be a good horse woman someday."

Some Indians were able to borrow money from Dad with no collateral, others often brought articles to hock when they needed money. Dad kept these transactions in a ledger he drolly called the Bank of Rock Creek records. We had beaded costumes, bags, moccasins, blankets, shawls, rifles, saddles and tack of all kinds in our care.

I never owned a saddle. There was usually one hanging in the shed for me to use; if not I rode bareback or used Dad's. I almost had a half interest in a saddle once..but that is a different story.

Word evidently got around that Ed Mattson would take horses on debts because soon we were snowed under with wild cayuses. We never had a bona-fide cowboy as a hired man so the horses remained unbroken.

We raised colts from the mares. The bay filly, Kentucky, was bred to Dewey Beeks' Arabian stallion. On March 19, 1946, she had the most wonderful little creature I had ever seen. My first colt! I named him Jiffi.

Jiffi & I get acquainted

By summer's end I had him halter broke and had suffered rope burnt hands, kicked shins, playful nips on my shoulders and fingers and crushed toes. Despite these injuries I loved every minute with him. Jiffi came running whenever he heard me bang on the feed can. Even a whistle would bring him if he was close enough to hear.

That winter when the horses came into the barn to be fed, I'd slip onto Jiffi's back while he ate. He became so accustomed to me there he paid no attention.

When branding time arrived the next spring, Dad decided I should ride Jiffi to the Hayes place. We started out being led behind Dad on Tony but before long he handed me the halter rope. Jiffi and I rode with the round-up crew like we'd done it all our lives. Dad looked back and grinned from time to time. I think he realized this was not an entirely new experience for us.

Probably in order to keep me from riding a green colt around the country that summer, the folks bought a white mare for me from Joe Hoctor. Dimples had been trained for the sheriff's posse drill team. I discovered she responded to knee pressure. We were soon doing fancy figure eights at top speed with no bridle, always in the lower pasture where we hoped Mom wouldn't spot us. Dimples and I rode many happy miles that summer but all the while I was dreaming of next year. Next year, I'd be riding Jiffi.

It was not to be. That fall Jiffi contracted distemper. I knew how dreaded the disease was, for one summer when I ran out of reading material I had read Dad's old veterinary book from cover to cover. Still, there was so much hope in my heart for him to live. I couldn't believe it when I returned from school one day and he was gone. It was a heartbreaking way for a 13 year old girl to learn that all stories do not have a happy ending.

ADVENTURES WITH NANCY

The first time Nancy and I went horseback riding together we decided to go to the Hayes place. This was my first ride since old Sam had kicked my teeth out seven years earlier. Sam was to be my mount today, which didn't do much for my morale. I waved bravely to Mom after listening to her instructions of "Be careful, ect." and hoped she wouldn't notice my shaking knees.

Me as Patsy Montana, in Daddy's boots

The ride down was uneventful. I found myself relaxing and enjoying the ride. Sam was docile as a kitten until I dismounted to open a gate and left the reins around his neck. Hadn't I seen movie cowboys do that? Sam had never seen a movie and didn't know he was supposed to stand patiently until I closed the gate. Off he trotted towards home.

Nancy leaned over with her hand stuck out and said "Jump up". She might as well have been hanging her hand from the moon. Her horse, Suzie, was a two year old colt but very big for her age and was not wearing a saddle. After several unsuccessful attempts to get on I was not at all sure I wanted to be there from the way Suzie was acting up. We finally maneuvered her near a fence post from where I took a flying leap and lit on her back. I breathed a little easier, at least I wouldn't have to walk home.

It soon became apparent Suzie would not tolerate being ridden double. After several wild antics I decided to walk home. I could tell Nancy was beginning to doubt my courage. She was barefooted so it was out of the question for her to take a turn walking.

Meanwhile old Sam kept plodding along in front of us and would *almost* let me catch him at times. His pace quickened considerably a half mile from home so he beat us there by several minutes. Poor Mom was frantic when we finally showed up.

MORE ADVENTURES WITH NANCY

The Cigar Episode
Some days were boring even at Nancy's house. Usually when this occurred, we'd tease her little cousin, Pat, who was temporarily living with the Stouts; but today her mother had gone somewhere taking Pat with her. In desperation we asked Nancy's sister Jean to play a game with us but she refused, telling us to be good because she was going up to her room to read.

Nancy and I had a lot in common. A snooty big sister with a neat bedroom upstairs was just one of them. Since the game we'd wanted to play was no fun with two people we sat on the davenport and plotted revenge.

Dave Stout did not smoke cigars, why was there one lying on the table? This gave us an idea!

In the kitchen a few minutes later, Nancy found a match and the key to Jean's room. We tiptoed up the stairs and locked her door. Jean heard the bolt click and asked us what we were up to. We giggled and said she'd soon find out. She gave a disgusted grunt. It was obvious she was trying to ignore us.

We lit the cigar and began to blow smoke through a wide crack under the door. We continued quite a while before Jean noticed the smell. It must have been a good book as the smoke was pretty thick on our side by then.

She came to the door, tried it, then threatened our lives if we didn't let her out. We puffed on.

Jean said she'd tell Mom. It didn't faze Nancy. She puffed faster. I was impressed! That threat always worked at home. Then Jean told us," You crazy kids will probably burn the house down." We puffed some more.

Soon we heard a muffled cough and the windows being opened. Oh, this was great! We puffed harder.

Finally, Jean said the windows were opened and the smoke was going outside so we might as well put the cigar out. It seemed like a good idea. It was getting short anyway and we were turning a bit green ourselves.

Even though our lives had been threatened we unlocked the door and peeked in. Jean was laughing! Imagine her laughing after we'd attempted to asphyxiate her. What a sport! Maybe big sisters were human after all.

I began to observe mine with hopeful eyes in hopes she,

too, might have this remarkable trait. In time I discovered
she did.

Milking the Mare

Everyone had a milk cow in those days. A special place
in the barn was equipped with a manger and a stanchion
where the cow stood to be milked. It was the coziest place
in the barn as the man who milked twice a day in all types
of weather had taken extra effort to build it that way. It
seemed a shame to let this nice part of the barn go unused
so much. I suppose that was our reasoning the day Nancy and
I decided to milk the mare.

With a little flake of hay it was easy to entice Suzie
to put her head in the stanchion. Nancy snapped the neck
brace shut. Before we could put our plan into action, Suzie
discovered she was caught and decided she didn't want to
be. With one mighty backwards jerk, half the stanchion
raised off the floor and went sailing out the opened door
around Suzies neck.

I'll never forget the wild scene of Suzie bucking and
kicking around the Stout's barnyard with pieces of the
stanchion flying off with every leap.

We finally calmed the poor frightened horse and removed
what little remained around her neck. We apologized to her.

If I remember correctly, we did a lot of apologizing for
that escapade. Not even a big sister who was human dared
laugh about that one for a long time.

SCHOOL DAYS AT ROOSEVELT

Roosevelt School and garage where we played anti-over

During the summer of 1939 I was given an exam to determine if I was ready to enroll in the first grade. I wouldn't be six until January but as there were no other children my age in the community, it seemed best I begin early so I'd have classmates.

I was not overjoyed to discover my classmates were five boys. The boys I had known up to now had either scared or teased me so badly I considered them all bothersome, noisy creatures to avoid. It took several months for me to relax and begin to think of them as friends. It's a miracle I learned anything during this period!

Our teacher, Mrs. Reader, somehow understood my adjustment problems and was exceptionally kind to me. I'm sure I wouldn't have made it if it hadn't been for her.

I tried to finish my work neatly, but quickly so I could play with a set of ceramic Snow White and Seven

Dwarfs figurines. I liked the set of cardboard farm animals, too, but of course the boys usually had them occupied. They sometimes let me play with the turkey.

Our reading lesson was conducted from a long bench where we all sat to take turns reading aloud about Alice and Jerry and their dog Spot. I wondered if we'd ever learn to read anything worthwhile. Frankly, I got tired of "Look! Look! See Jerry run!". By the time third grade rolled around I had exhausted the reading material in the primary room and began checking out books from the Intermediate room. I enjoyed, "Susanna, the Pioneer Cow", the Wizard of Oz series and the Adventures of Poppy, a fairy who tried to live in a dollhouse but kept breaking the cardboard furniture whenever she sat down.

We'd gather at the piano each morning to sing. Occasionally, I still find myself singing, "Come On Black Pony" or "October Morning" that I learned then. One of the boys requested "There Is A Tavern In The Town" several times a week. I suspect the teacher wished it hadn't been included in the book, but it was the one we sang the loudest. Everyone knew the words to that one.

When something was needed from the store, everyone's hands flew up as volunteers. Bud Reader's store was a friendly place. The glass in the door rattled gently behind

Marilynn, Denise & I waiting for the bus

you as you stepped onto the oiled floor. After cheerful greetings were exchanged with Bud, the stuffed birds that perched on the high shelves of the room got a few minutes attention before business was transacted. I never knew there were so many different kinds of ducks! Before leaving, a visit to the black and white cat was in order. He spent his time sleeping on the paper sacks in back of the store and seemed to appreciate a pat on the head.

Every year Mrs. Reader gave each of her students a birthday party. She served a cake, complete with candles and sometimes, jello. A gift and card signed, Mrs. Reader and Bud, with a quarter tucked in, were always part of the day. The quarter was usually slid across the counter in Bud's store for a candy bar later in the week. A quarter could buy 5 candy bars at that time.

Elam "Ollie" Binns was the bus driver who ruled with an iron hand. He impressed us one afternoon when he stopped and made his son, Ronald, walk home after he had ignored a 'sit down and behave yourself' command. From then on, just a glance in the large interior rear view mirror and seeing Ollie looking at you was enough to make one sit down and behave.

Doris Miller rode her horse, Coaly, to the school bus. There was a shed at the Gately place where he spent the day waiting for her return. The Tynan kids were not so fortunate; they walked. This was the only 'visible' poor family in the community. It is said they lived on squash one winter. Mom would sometimes put extra food in my lunch pail to share with them.

Coyotes were so scarce in the country, the morning we spotted one from the bus windows was red letter day. It might have been a lion for the excitement it created.

The games we played during recess were Mother, May I; Blackman, Tag and Jumping rope. I once skipped hot pepper one hundred times and could have done more but the teacher made me stop. There was the usual playground equipment outside and wonderful rock formations where we played house. We invented a game of Cowboys and Indians in which we ran around the school house shooting each other. The Indian kids always wanted to be the Indians. Anti-Over, over the bus garage and basketball were favorite sports as I grew older.

Mrs. Glass became my teacher in the sixth grade. We began to learn about the history of our country. After we had studied the battle of

Front Row - Delbert Tynan, Violet Tynan, Dolores Hamilton, Carol Binns, Gary Olson, Warner Jim, Jimmy Symonds. Back Row - Billy Marvel, Bruce Sanders, Connie Beeks, Beverly Mattson, Mrs. Reader

the little bighorn, Mrs. Glass left us with the statement, "It is questionable who was right." It was the first time I realized our government could possibly be wrong.

Mrs. Glass became ill and left during my seventh year
at school. Mrs. Coleman was hired
to take her place. For some
reason, none of us had respect for
our new teacher. We spent our days
taking turns deviling her. For no
apparent reason she'd suddenly
turn to me, shake her finger and
say, "And you, Beverly Mattson,
sitting there grinning like a
Cheshire cat!"

I don't remember what provoked
the battle between Nancy and Mrs.
Coleman. By the time I realized
something was wrong, the teacher
had jerked Nancy from her desk by

*~Mrs. Reader, Mrs. Dodson &
Mrs. Glass~*

the pigtails and was escorting her towards the door at
arm's length while Nancy kicked and screamed at the top of
her lungs. The last words we heard as the door slammed
behind them was Nancy's threat, "My Dad's on the school
board! He'll get you for this!"

The entire school was soon in turmoil as the other
teachers came to restore peace and kids popped their heads

in our door wanting to know what had happened. We certainly had the liveliest room in school that year!

When we returned for the eighth grade, a new teacher, Mrs. Miller greeted us. Nancy's folks had separated during the summer and she had gone to live with her mother. I was lost!

I spent Halloween night with a new girl in school, Virginia Alstreberg. As a friend of hers drove us around town we decided it was too quiet and needed some pepping up. The first prank we pulled was dumping cans on the railroad stations platform; then an outhouse was tipped over as Phyllis Seely glanced out the door and wailed, "There goes our toilet!" We probably soaped the store windows, too.

The next morning, Mrs. Miller began the day with the statement, "While some of you were creating mischief last night, someone else stacked my firewood in the woodshed." It wasn't difficult to see who had done the good deed, for Warner Jim was beaming. My stomach hurt; I was not proud of what I'd had a hand in.

The high school by that time had dwindled to girls only. They decided to hold a junior prom. When I asked Mom if I could wear a formal and attend, her answer surprised me – for once it was yes! If I remember correctly, the dress was a hand me down from Denise but as it was a beautiful turquoise blue with short puffy sleeves, I didn't mind. Every spare moment at home was spent learning to walk in high heels. Mom had taught us to walk with a book on our head for posture's sake so I wasn't satisfied until I could teeter across the room in my new shoes balancing a book.

The anticipation of the dance was overwhelming! To my distress, Clarence Kelley and I accidentally bumped heads on the bus the night before the big event. As I feared, my first formal and first black eye occurred simultaneously.

The prom turned out to be only mildly successful. Since only a few of the girls had dates they had to depend on the crowd for dance partners. A group of young Mexican section hands who were temporarily working near town were about the only unattached men who came; much to the discomfort of the mothers.

The next year began with Warner, Virginia, Jean Stout and myself as high school students with Mr. Goude as our teacher. Jean had enough credits to graduate in mid-term. Virginia soon quit school to marry the assistant custodian at the school, Loren Lester. Warner only came to school on cold days, or when he felt like it. When my freshman year ended, the door on Roosevelt High School was locked and the key thrown away.

The next year, high school students were transferred to Arlington.

CHRISTMAS SEASON AT SCHOOL

Each year when we returned to school from Thanksgiving vacation we began practicing for the Christmas Program. In my 1939 acting debut I portrayed a doll. My part was to walk stiffly across the stage calling, "Mama! Mama!" It wasn't a great performance, for even though I had long curls no one likened me to Shirley Temple.

Mrs. Reader always sent a copy of the play home with us to read before she assigned the parts. One year I craved the part of Allison, a rich visiting cousin. The next day I was thrilled to be named Allison, despite the fact a boy kissed me under the mistletoe at the end of the play. It wouldn't have been so bad except the boy who got that part was one I couldn't stand! I made the best of it – I'd do anything to please Mrs. Reader.

The day we drew names at school was always exciting. We tried to keep the secret whose name we had drawn but it was difficult. In a few days everyone thought they knew who had who's name. It was a lingering game until the packages were opened and the mystery solved at last.

During play practice there were distractions backstage while we awaited our cue. We enjoyed snooping through boxes of costumes that were stored there. Sometimes the cast was disturbed when we tried on some ridiculous piece and couldn't suppress our giggles.

The passageway behind the stage was covered with names. We recognized some of the names of grown-ups we knew. If they had been brave enough to leave their names there, we would too. It was the only place at school one dared write on the walls.

The night of the performance arrived all too quickly! We'd peek through the curtains and wish so many people hadn't come to watch. Stage fright was always worse before the curtain parted.

Following the plays Santa arrived carrying sacks containing nuts, hard candy, and orange and a popcorn ball for everyone. The floor under the big tree was piled high with gifts, for it was planned that no one was to leave empty handed. Santa called out the name on each gift, then the older children distributed them to the crowd. Our parents received presents we had made from clay. They were sometimes puzzled as to what it was supposed to be but were always pleased, nonetheless.

Having an older sister who told me there was no such thing as a REAL Santa, I was in on the secret early that Bud Reader was under the Santa suit. If there had been an Oscar presented for the most outstanding performance of the evening, Bud would have won it every year.

Even though we had to return the next day to dismantle the tree, the ride home from the play officially ended the Christmas season at school. It was nice to relax in the backseat after experiencing the most exciting evening of the year. The folks remarked how well we'd done, even if a sour note had escaped or a line was temporarily forgotten. They had been proud of us, regardless.

We felt smug in the fact we had known all along who had our name, but somehow that gift never surpassed the one received from Mrs. Reader; it was always something I treasured and wanted to keep forever.

SUNDAY SCHOOL

Mom took us to Roosevelt almost every week to attend Sunday school classes at the school building. It seemed strange to have a teacher other than Mrs. Reader.

In 1941 at Easter, when I was 4 or 5, a minister was asked to perform baptisms at a sunrise service. The congregation gathered on the flat near Seely's spring. I suppose it was water from here that our heads were sprinkled with. I was disappointed I didn't feel more holy after being baptized but Mom seemed relieved it was done.

Me with a favorite flower, the bleeding heart

The evening before the big event the Sunday school teachers had gone to the spring to hide dozens of Easter eggs. Imagine their surprise when only a few were found. It seems the ravens had either stayed up late or had gotten up very early to feast on them. I didn't find one!

A MUSICIAN WAS I

After the jews harp mysteriously
disappeared a long procession of musical
instruments followed. A hired man whose name
I remember only as Red, gave me his old
violin. My violinist career ended quickly
when I left it on the lawn overnight while
it was raining. It fell into several pieces
when I picked it up.

"Practice makes perfect" our mother told us

Mrs. Reader gave free piano lessons to
anyone who wanted them at school and I took
my turn. After learning the scales, the first song in the
book was…"Do you see boys up there in the hay? No, I can't
see, I'm not looking that way." Hardly any could be
inspired to play songs as silly as that! I liked it a
little better when I learned "Bill Grogan's Goat"; but
still, piano playing just wasn't me. After two tortuous
years of practice and missing morning recess once a week,
Mom let me quit because I was so miserable.

Several years later, Denise and Jean Stout began trying
to organize a dance band and needed a drummer. Mom probably
thought if she had to chaperone the girls to dances anyway,
I might as well join them. Mrs. Reader was going to

Portland and offered to look into the price of a used drum
set. It wasn't long until I was the proud owner of a
marvelous Ludwig set which included a gray bass drum
trimmed in sparkly silver bands, two tom-toms painted with
chinese dragons, a snare drum and all sorts of accessories.

I tried to learn from a drum music book but finally
gave up and just played. Luckily, I must have had a natural
sense of rhythm because I was accepted into the band.

The three of us played for dances at Roosevelt, Dot and
Bickleton grange halls and the old Cleveland school house.
The latter was a decrepit building that had been vacant for
years. I was leery of hitting the cymbal hard there for
fear the ceiling would fall down around us.

The first New Years dance we played at I was amazed at
how people celebrated! This experience was a real eye
opener into the world of fun and frolic.

I met many young people from Bickleton and the
surrounding areas. I found out later that they envied me
and all the while I had been jealous of their freedom to
dance any time they wanted to. Johnnie Beeks enjoyed
filling in for me several times during the evening so I
learned to dance and discovered I loved it. I even thought
of becoming a professional dancer but couldn't see how it
could be worked into my ranch in Texas so dropped that

desire.

After several years of being a professional musician I retired when Denise got a job playing with a dance band from Goldendale.

On one of our rare journeys to Sunnyside, Mom spotted a used trumpet in a store window. I don't remember having a burning wish to own it but I spent the summer learning to play the trumpet from an "Easy To Learn" book from the catalog. When I entered Arlington High School and joined the band, I was immediately put in first chair: so the "Easy To Learn" book must have been a good teacher. The folks soon bought me a classy new King coronet and my era of used instruments was over. I enjoy telling people I played horn in the same band as Doc Severingson, but am careful not to mention he left Arlington long before I made the scene.

BLISTERS & FRUSTRATION

When Mom complained about the birds eating the cherries, Dad's solution was to teach me to shoot the .22 rifle. It was an old Remington automatic that shot very straight. Soon the English sparrow population was drastically reduced. The cats followed me around the ranch like I was the pied piper of Hamlin, knowing soon they'd be dining on fat sparrows.

One fall Dad returned from town with a .30-.30 rifle for me. I think he had won it on a punch board. Mom was totally disgusted with him for giving me such a gift. She should have been used to it; I was. Over the years Dad made stilts and carved wooden six guns for me, while Denise had received doll houses, cupboards and toy ironing boards he had made. This arrangement had always suited me and I was thrilled with the new rifle, especially when I was invited to go deer hunting!

When I mentioned at school I was going hunting, a friend, Don Archer remarked he'd like to go. Arrangements were made and on the big day, he appeared packing his .22 to shoot gray diggers with. It was the last day of the season and Dad had already got his deer, so he carried a shotgun in hopes a grouse might cross our path. We were a motley threesome; hardly a threat to any deer!

We drove to Whites Creek and spent the day walking up one canyon and down the next without seeing a single deer. We were nearing the pickup to start home when I spotted one across the canyon. When I finally convinced Dad it had horns and was safe to shoot at, the buck had moved up the hill farther away. I don't think he ever saw us as the wind was blowing like a banshee and carried our scent away from him. My first shot was low; the next one high; the next one in front of him, and so on until the gun was empty and the deer had disappeared over the hill. It had been a large buck. He had been a much bigger target than a sparrow. Why had I missed him? I was to ask myself this same question many times in the years that followed. Although my deer tag went unattached during those years I still enjoyed my outings despite the blisters and frustration. During the season, Dad and I would leave early Saturday morning for a quick hunt. One morning I missed two bucks. It was difficult to eat in the cook house and take the jibs from the hired men after that fiasco! I hope I took their teasing in a sportsmanlike manner. I tried to.

On Sundays, most of the crew went hunting with us. It began to rain one day after we had driven far up Squaw Creek. The hunting prospects looked good and no one gave a thought to the primitive road we had come over. By the time we left, the road had become a quagmire. The pickup was a

three speed International that was known as a gutless
wonder even in good weather. Oh, how we could have used a
4-wheel drive vehicle that day! We slipped and slid and
pushed until we were covered with mud and so tired we could
drop. I've never been so glad to see Newell Creek and the
graveled road in my life!

I was lost in the woods a good part of the time.
Whenever this happened I'd sit on a point until I caught a
glimpse of one of the parties. We seldom saw anyone else. I
spotted a cougar across the canyon one day while lost. It
was the only one I've seen in the wild. Another time a herd
of wild horses came out of the mist toward me. The leader
was a beautiful chestnut; the type Harrison Ridge was
famous for. There were many dilapidated homestead shacks
tucked in the woods with a lot of interesting junk lying
around. I never took a souvenir because I wanted my hands
free in case I saw the retarded buck I was convinced had to
be hiding somewhere.

The longest hike I took was with Ed Morris. Dad let us
out at Wood Gulch and picked us up at the Dot grange hall
that afternoon. I didn't see a deer, but Ed who was ahead
of me(he was always ahead of me) saw some does. I had
blisters on top of blisters that night. I never got around
to buying a decent pair of hunting boots. As if I didn't
take enough punishment during deer season, when Dad asked

if I wanted to go elk hunting I said sure. We went to the
Cowiche area above Yakima to wallow in snow above our knees
and see no elk. We stayed with Jackie and Art Humphreys
and had a nice visit, even though the hunt was a failure.

The drive home across the Simcoes was frightful! Trucks
lay in the ditch and those vehicles that were moving were
doing so slowly, with chains. By
this time we had a jeep and it
chugged through in fine style.
I'm sure Dad's palms were
sweaty; mine were.

I'm glad to say I didn't
quit hunting until I got one,
even if it happened after I was
married. Dad and I were hunting
together the day I finally found
the retarded buck. I was proud
to show Dad, at last, I could do
it!

Me and the retarded buck

FROM ONION SOUP TO SLIM PICKENS

I couldn't wait to become old enough to join the 4-H

cooking club. It appeared the members had a good time staying after school for meetings. At my first meeting, I learned it was not all fun and games. Our project that day was making potato soup. Cy Beeks, the leader, asked if I could peel a potato. When I confessed I couldn't, the older girls looked at me in amazement. In answer to the next question, I said, "Sure, I can peel an onion," wondering to myself just how it was done. I struggled with the onions while the tears that trickled down my cheeks were not all caused from the fumes. I was miserable, besides, I didn't like potato soup and the thought of eating it later didn't seem like much of a reward. I was really out of my league in the cooking class but I persevered through several years of it.

I finally convinced Dad I needed a 4-H steer. We drove the pickup to Condon in search of a likely show steer. We visited several ranches but the good steers had already been chosen by local 4-H members. We were really disappointed on our ride back to Arlington when Dad happened to think of Ike Weatherford's ranch nearby. Ike had a steer that might do, so we drove across the pasture in the dark to have a look. It was him or nothing. I named him Olex. The steer bloated often and was off feed so much he wasn't fat enough to take to the fair that fall.

I was not discouraged. I had learned that feeding steers was much more fun than peeling onions. From then on I fattened steers we raised on the ranch. Although I never won a blue ribbon, the experiences at the fair and Pacific International Exposition where I showed them were reward enough. The money was nice, too.

We slept in a girls dormitory on the grounds while we attended the P.I. One woman looked after all of us, which was a hopeless task as there were probably a hundred of us.

A rodeo and horse show was held in conjunction with the P.I. The kids from Klickitat County became friends with Slim Pickens. He was the rodeo clown and contestant in the bulldogging event at the time. He later appeared in movies for Walt Disney and other films in Hollywood. We'd visit with Slim every morning at the horse stalls. He always had some yarn to share with us and even let some of the boys ride his horse around the arena. At the rodeo when the bull riding event neared, the orchestra played the Matador Song. That was Slim's cue to enter the arena dressed in his matador costume, twirling a cape and executing fancy bull fighting techniques. He was hero material if I ever saw it!

On the day our steers were to be sold, we girls dressed in our best western clothes and fixed our hair as best we could. Some of the boys thought we had an advantage over them so they asked Syb Kayser and I if we'd take their steers through the sales ring, hoping to get a few cents more. We led some pretty fancy steers through the sale that year, smiling at the prospective buyers and being as showy as we could.

After the steer was sold, He was led directly to the slaughter pens behind the building. It was a brutal experience to say goodbye to a four-legged friend in that manner. The first year when I led Stub to the pen, I was thankful it was raining so no one would notice my tears. He had won 6th place in the medium weight class that year which was the largest class. The next year my steer had placed 13th in his class and had not been so gentle. It was easy to slip off the halter and turn away. Perhaps my heart was growing harder.

During my early years of 4-H, camp was held west of Trout Lake at Peterson Prairie. We visited the ice caves, found a few early huckleberries to eat and waded in the icy water. We made new friends to correspond with and by fair time, greeted them like old friends when we met again.

Five or six girls from our club went to camp together one year. It was held in late July which was the hot period at home. We were surprised to discover the extra blanket Mom had included in our bedroll was welcome. Dad insisted we bring a tent. We were determined it would be unused but we put it up to please him. One night we were awakened by a noise none of us had heard before. We decided to finish the night in the tent. It was all over camp the next morning that a cougar had screamed nearby. I think we all silently thanked Dad for having the foresight to send the tent. We used it every night from then on.

One year, Toppy Shattuck, our beef leader, put some hay

My first trip to 4-H camp was when Mom delivered these girls. I was too young to stay. I ate my first huckleberry the day this photo was taken. This is at Peterson Prairie in Trout Lake Wash. Connie Beeks, Carol Binns, Me, Denise and Audry Bundy

bales in his truck and picked up kids from Bickleton, Roosevelt and Goldendale and delivered us to camp. We were all close friends by the time we arrived. Camaraderie comes easy when everybody has a dirty face!

When camp was moved to Smokey Creek, a few miles further up the road, two huge tents were provided for sleeping quarters. We played serious baseball for recreation. Dad had taught me the fundamentals of the catcher position as he had caught on a team that played the Indians every Sunday when he was a young man. I held that position on my team at camp. It wasn't always easy to hang tight behind the batters as I was playing with the big kids now and the pitcher didn't hold back. I suffered some nasty bruises and a broken little finger but I wouldn't have changed positions for anything.

I was walking through the woods one day with a small group, when we discovered a cave with a huge entrance. When we showed the counselors, they decided to have a wiener roast there that night for the entire camp. The fires were lit and the wieners being removed from their packages when we realized the smoke was not rising but billowing around us in clouds. We all headed outside with tears streaming from our eyes. Some of the smaller kids got sick. So much for the wiener roast!

Evenings spent around a campfire under the trees, singing and roasting marshmallows were more successful. It was here I received my first "grown up" kiss. Paul was a good baseball player and enjoyed roasting marshmallows for me. It was only natural I'd be attracted to him. When the spontaneous kiss occurred, his glasses slid down his nose and we both ended up laughing. So much for romance at 4-H camp!

ARLINGTON, MY HOME TOWN

When wind and atmospheric conditions were favorable,

Arlington's noon siren served us at Roosevelt as well. Arlington was less than a mile away yet, before September 1948, the times I had been there could be counted on one hand. The Columbia River created a mighty barrier between the two towns. A person had to have urgent business to cross the river, or at least it seemed so.

Urgent business became a reality to me when during the summer the school board informed us they had closed the high school and made arrangements for students to attend in Arlington. I greeted this news with mixed feelings. It would be nice to have classmates again but I wouldn't know any of them! Although other students from Roosevelt would be attending, none were in my class. So with high hopes, yet with fears I might not be accepted, I faced my new life.

In 1948, Arlington was a shady town of a bit more than 600 people. It is probably best remembered by the locust trees that lined the streets. The trees were scarred, fender high by generations of drivers who misjudged their parallel parking abilities. The trees towered above the two tallest buildings in town, the Welcome and Vendome hotels. There were cottonwoods, too, on the side streets. On windy spring days, their cottony fluffs blow around corners and into the main street.

During this era the town was enjoying an upsurge of population and economy. Two large machinery companies served the surrounding

wheat growing community. Three car dealerships, eight gas stations, seven restaurants, a snack shop and two grocery stores attested to the fact of the town in a boom.

The town also contained Doc Wilhelm's drug store, a laundry, the Rio theater, Hurt's hardware, the Pastime tavern, a feed store, barber and beauty shops, a liquor store, McClaskey's auto court, Eleonor's dress shop and Addie's Antiques.

An Oregon State Police unit, the railroad depot, a grain elevator, the Bank of Eastern Oregon, and a telephone office all employed a number of people. Three churches, city offices, the post office and the Masonic Hall helped fill up the gaps in town.

There were five or six apartment complexes. Most of

these were above the business houses along Main Street. The largest unit, known by the unprestigious name of Dogpatch, was located south of town.

Overlooking all of this, from the sidehill, was the imposing brick school building with long flights of steps leading up to it. This was my first destination.

THE NEW KID

Unfortunately, I was the only 'new kid' that year among the fourteen of us in the sophomore class. It was uncomfortable to know everyone was watching me carefully. When the boy sitting behind me in history class accidently splattered ink on my white blouse, I kept my cool but my first impression of Dick Wheelhouse was hardly love at first sight! The ink stain never completely washed out. Perhaps it was his method of branding me.

As weeks went by, I found myself too busy to worry if I'd be accepted. I played cornet in the band, sang alto in the glee club, marched with the drill team and tried out for the class play. To my surprise I got the leading part! My mama doll experience from 1939 was finally paying off.

While waiting to become 'one of the girls', studying got all my attention. The teachers probably thought they had a real student on their hands. My first six weeks term grades were high but soon dropped back to average after I became acquainted. I thought there were better things to do than study all the time. I was on the honor roll once. Mom offered me $5.00 if I could make it and the need for money was great.

HORSES, TOWNS PEOPLE AND A PRINCES

Nobody could call Arlington a one-horse town and get away with it. The Saddle Club was very active and seemed to be 'the thing' to belong to. At first I was puzzled why town people without cows needed a horse but I was soon to learn about trail rides and competing in horse shows, etc. The organization's main function was to sponsor an annual rodeo the first weekend in May.

When the girls in my class made me aware of the upcoming rodeo and queen contest, it seemed only natural to try for it. There were rules to obey. First, you must find a sponsor, preferably a business in town where one would hope they'd sell tickets for you, because the girl who sold the most became queen. Contestants must wear black gambler striped pants and a white shirt and hat.(The official costume of the saddle club). The girls from town knew who to get as sponsors so by the time I had a chance to look, all the good ones were taken. I wish I could remember who suggested Roy Phillippi to me..someone did. Lester Wheelhouse pre-arranged a meeting for us. I don't know why Roy, a boisterous, fun-loving man, and I, a shy quiet girl hit it off so well. Perhaps we were bound together through our love of horses. When the other girls learned who my sponsor was they were envious. They informed me he didn't sponsor just any girl for queen. For thirty years afterwards whenever we met he'd hollar, "By gosh, we just about beat 'em!'

That statement pretty well tells the story. Jean Kumm became queen because her sponsor, the owner of pastime, learning he was behind at the last minute, dashed to the tavern and sold seven tickets. Roy felt worse than I did, I'm sure. My reward was riding his splendid horse, Nelson in the grand entry as a princess. Jean, who was showing off to some cowboys before the show, fell from her horse and was probably the only queen with a dirty shirt hanging onto the saddle horn Arlington ever had. We all hated her for weeks, despite her difficulties. It was here I learned losing is sometimes a virtue.

A TYPICAL WEEKEND

There was nothing typical about a weekend in Arlington.

There were a variety of lifestyles, depending on who I stayed with. I went to church with the Methodists when I stayed with Pat Desler. Her dad even drove us in on Saturday to attend Reverend Hitchcock's bible study. The Reverend was a woman who tried valiantly to save our little souls. Although her meetings were open to all teenagers, it remained a female group. She was always urging us to get some boys to attend. We never succeeded.

My favorite weekends were those I spent with Jeri Austin. Her folks owned the Welcome Hotel and coffee shop. Saturday mornings were occupied with cleaning the apartment. After our job was inspected and approved, (rarely on the first attempt) the day was ours to do with as we pleased. After liberally sprinkling ourselves with her mother's Channel #5 perfume, we stepped out on the town.

Occasionally we went to Addie's Antique shop to look around. We had no intention of buying anything and she knew it so we didn't bother her often. Who would want this queer old stuff? We sometimes giggled at the sheer absurdity of it. From Addie's we'd meander down the street to Eleonor's. Buying clothes made a lot more sense to us.

Eleonor knew what looked good on every woman in town and did her buying with individuals in mind. The first time I really felt accepted in Arlington was the day she greeted me with, "I thought you might like this, Beverly." She was right. I did, and bought it.

After tomboying all over town we might head to the Oasis and listen to Jo Stafford sing "Slow Boat To China" or Hank Williams wail "The Lovesick Blues" on the jukebox, we might declare this a perfect day for a horseback ride. Roy Wheelhouse was the man in town to see about this. Roy was in partnership in the Ford Garage and Shell Oil distributing plant with Art Smythe. Imagine my surprise to learn his dad and uncle had once owned <u>our</u> Smythe Place. What a small world it was!

Garry's Hooty & Me in the dress from Eleonor's

Roy grew accustomed to loaning us his horses and seemed happy to have them exercised; but I learned the rascal couldn't always be trusted. One day he saddled up a new horse for me. She was a cute little crooked legged mare by the name of Molly Pouch. Molly and I explored south of town in a hurry that day. If there were junipers, rock piles and ditches she couldn't dodge in time we sailed over them!

After she tired she was easier to handle but a more wild ride I'd never taken. Jeri and I saw very little of each other. We both wondered if we'd really enjoyed the day.

Later, when Roy asked me how I like his new horse, I admitted she didn't rein very well. He laughed and said, "Well, what do you expect? It's only the second time she's been ridden."

The evening's entertainment during a weekend in Arlington depended on the season. During the winter months it meant a basketball game, or if summer prevailed and there was no dance somewhere that weekend, a short walk to the Rio was on the agenda. It didn't matter what was playing.. we went regardless.

THE FERRY

No story of Arlington or Roosevelt would be complete without mentioning the ferry which Ben Flippen ran faithfully between the two towns for years. His hours were

from 7am to 10pm daily. The schedule will remain in my mind
forever. I spent half my teenage years either waiting for
the ferry to pick me up or rushing for it to carry me home
at night. That dam ferry caused me more grief during my
life in Arlington than anything else.

Waiting for the !%#&%@! ferry, Arlington side

Enough has been said about it.

A LONG COLD WINTER

The winter of 1948-49 was a long hard one. In January
the river froze solid. Suddenly, I was stranded in
Arlington. The Welcome Hotel became home base for the next
six weeks. When people in town heard of my situation, many

of them invited me to their homes for meals and overnight stays. At first it proved fun to be on my own but as weeks went by homesickness set in so I appreciated being able to share some family life, even if it wasn't my own.

Mom wrote about frozen water pipes, power outages, blizzards and drifting snow at the ranch. They were fighting to keep the cattle fed and quite frankly, for their own survival. Meantime, while being quite comfortable in my hotel room, I didn't entirely escape the winter.

One night while a group of us skated on the river, Ben Weatherell fell through the ice. Horror turned to relief when it was discovered he had fallen into an air pocket and was alright. This made us realize our pastime was dangerous. It was discontinued.

There were days when school was canceled because the buses could not get through or the temperature was too cold to venture out safely. The gorge highway was closed many times, causing the town to be without the usual business at gas stations, restaurants and hotels.

One Saturday the weather looked good, so Jeri and I took the bus to Pendleton to shop. We had both been saving our money for new white bucks and couldn't live another day without them. We bought the shoes, then of course went to

Hamleys to inspect everything in the store. We had time to kill as our bus didn't leave for hours. We enjoyed a leisure dinner then went to see "Battleground", the latest Van Johnson movie. The movie had barely started when my leisure dinner began to feel strange in my stomach. The evening was spent rushing between the restroom to throw up and my seat to get a glimpse of Van on the screen. Luckily, Jeri had ordered differently from the menu.

Later, when we checked in at the bus depot, the man said, "The road to Arlington is locked up tight as a drum". I've always thought it was an odd way to say the buses weren't running because of the blizzard. The two of us scraped the bottom of our purses to come up with 10 cents so we could call Jeri's folks. Imagine receiving a phone call like this;
"Hi, Mom. We're still in Pendleton. The buses aren't running because of the storm. Bev is sick. We've spent all our money. What should we do?"

Miraculously, the solution was simple. The Austin's knew the owner of the Temple Hotel and called to say their daughter and a friend would be there shortly. We were given a nice room for the night and then next morning returned to Arlington wearing our new white bucks and giggling about our adventure.

It would seem we were not the only victims of the storm because after the highway through the Gorge had been closed for some time, word had come up from Claugh's Service station that a car had gotten through. I went along with some other kids to see.

There were two young men in a new Ford encrusted with ice, telling a gathering crowd about their harrowing experience. It is said everyone had 15 minutes of fame in their lifetime. This might have been it for these guys.

It was quite a while before anyone else made it through the Gorge, as I recall.

Finally, the winter eased and the ice began to break up on the river. My folks heard, somehow, that Deke Clark was taking a motorboat to Arlington to pick up his sister, Lois from the bus depot. They made arrangements for me to hitch a ride. If they had known how many icebergs there were out there, they may not have done so. The Titanic's demise crossed my mind several times. My job was to watch for the larger ones. We made it fine. I think by Monday, Ben Flippen decided the river was safe enough for the ferry to cross because I don't remember returning on the motorboat.

Even my two little nephews were glad to see me when I

finally returned home. Keith had learned to walk while I was gone and Garry chattered to me nonstop. Oh, it was great to be home again!

KABOOM!

One event that stands out in my mind as I lived in Arlington was not a humorous one. A peaceful Sunday morning erupted when the Oregon Trail restaurant exploded, breaking most of the windows on Main street. Fortunately, the restaurant was closed because the roof was blown off the building. An employee had neglected to close a gas valve on the stove the night before. The shattered lobby windows at the Welcome were deeply embedded into the leather chairs where I often sat to read. It was a miracle no one was injured.

PRECIOUS SCHOOL DAYS

During lunch break on the first warm spring day following the long winter, someone declared it too nice to return to school. The idea snowballed and kids scattered to the four winds. When the bell rang, only three students greeted the faculty. I don't remember the speech Mr. Ditto gave us the next day but it was effective because we never(almost)unanimously played hooky again.

The next two years went by so fast, I hardly had time to go home. In addition to the activities of my first year; the Honker staff, mixed chorus and the sextet took even more of my time and energy. I helped decorate class floats for May Day parades, acted in the Senior play and was part of the committee who planned the Junior prom. The theme was "South Pacific', from the Broadway play that made such a hit that year.

This prom proved to be more exciting than my previous ones. I didn't have a black eye; then too, the boy I had wanted to go with last year remembered to ask me early so I wouldn't have to go with someone else. When we left the hotel where I was staying with Jeri, he ushered me to a black Studebaker convertible waiting at the curb. I felt like Cinderella Being whisked off to the ball. Dick didn't always have a car. What he drove depended on what his dad had at the garage. What luck to have someone trade in such a car at prom time! Unlike Cinderella, I didn't lose my slipper that evening but I began to feel my heart slipping away. (Funny thing about this…the car was gone in a few days but my heart has felt the same for 34 years.)

BIG CHANGE ON THE WAY

One day we noticed the buildings on main street wore John Day Dam stickers. They were placed where the pool level would be when the dam was completed. The government was giving early warning as change would take place. We shrugged our shoulders and thought it impossible for the river to reach these heights.

It took many years and untold dollars for the Corps of Engineers to prove they had been right all along. The old town came tumbling down and a new one rebuilt further south.

Though the Arlington I knew is gone now, it will always remain in my heart as the place this farm girl called her 'home town'. Even a dam can't drown memories.

The End

Home and the center of my whole world